CIVIL RIGHTS IN AMERICA

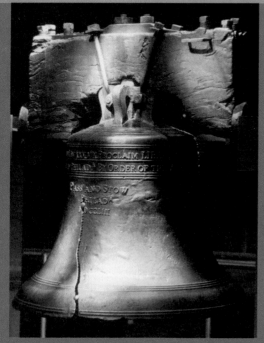

The Liberty Bell

WRITTEN BY RICK BEARD

Copyright 2016 by Eastern National
470 Maryland Drive, Suite 1, Fort Washington, PA 19034
Visit us at www.eParks.com

The America's National Parks Press series is produced by Eastern National, a not-for-profit partner of the National Park Service. Our mission is to promote the public's understanding and support of America's national parks and other public trust partners by providing quality educational experiences, products, and services.

ISBN 978-1-59091-178-5

W*e hold these truths to be self-evident, that all men are created equal, that they are endowed by their Creator with certain unalienable Rights, that among these are Life, Liberty and the pursuit of Happiness.*

—Declaration of Independence

July 1776

The men who signed the Declaration of Independence in the summer of 1776 proclaimed a vision of equality that continues to inspire millions of people. But there can be little doubt that the delegates gathered in Philadelphia did not intend to extend these "unalienable Rights" to the more than 500,000 African Americans living in their midst, the vast majority of whom were enslaved. For the next 225 years, a large part of the American story chronicles how African Americans fought to realize the promise of the Declaration of Independence.

The newly independent Americans did little to resolve the inherent contradiction between their democratic ideals and the realities of slavery. When the delegates convened in 1787 to draft the U.S. Constitution, they reached a consensus only after a series of compromises that further embedded chattel slavery in the new nation's social and economic fabric. For the purposes of representation and taxation, each slave was to be counted as three-fifths of a person; the slave trade was protected from prohibition until 1808; and states were obligated to return fugitive slaves to their owners.

Many of the founders expected slavery to disappear over time, but just the opposite proved true. Between 1790 and 1860, the slave population

Left: Thomas Jefferson, 3rd president of the United States, stipple engraving by Cornelius Tiebout, ca. 1801.

grew to include 3,953,760. At the same time, the nearly 500,000 free blacks living in the United States witnessed the steady erosion of those few rights they had enjoyed. In 1852, the fiery abolitionist Frederick Douglass denounced slavery as "the great sin and shame of America!"

> *Neither slavery nor involuntary servitude, except as a punishment for crime whereof the party shall have been duly convicted, shall exist within the United States, or any place subject to their jurisdiction.*
>
> —Thirteenth Amendment, 1865
> U.S. Constitution
> Ratified December 1865

In 1857, the Supreme Court validated Douglass' grim analysis, ruling in the case of *Dred Scott v. Sandford* that because neither enslaved nor free African Americans could be American citizens, they had no standing to sue in federal court. Furthermore, the federal government had no power to regulate slavery in any territory acquired after 1789. Writing for the majority, Chief Justice Roger Taney judged blacks "altogether unfit to associate with the white race, either in social or political relations, and so far inferior that they had no rights which the white man was bound to respect."

Virginia slave auction, English wood engraving, 1861.

First reading of the Emancipation Proclamation before President Abraham Lincoln's cabinet, color engraving, 1866.

Today considered one of the worst decisions in the Supreme Court's history, the Dred Scott ruling had an inflammatory effect on a national political scene already deeply divided over slavery's future. Abraham Lincoln condemned the decision, observing that the "ultimate destiny" of blacks in the United States "has never appeared so hopeless as in the last three or four years." His election as president three years later quickly led to southern secession and the outbreak of war.

Within a year of the shelling of Fort Sumter, the actions of the Union government made it increasingly apparent that slavery would not outlive · a northern victory. By mid-1862, Congress had done away with slavery in the District of Columbia and all current and future territories. On New Year's Day 1863, President Lincoln signed the Emancipation Proclamation, abolishing slavery in all those areas controlled by the Confederacy. And after a bruising political battle, Congress passed the Thirteenth Amendment, ending slavery in January 1865.

Abraham Lincoln did not live to see this amendment ratified, nor was he able to steer the nation through the initial years of Reconstruction, a period during which African Americans enjoyed a tantalizing brush with political power. The adoption of the Fourteenth Amendment in 1868 undid the Dred Scott decision, affirming African American citizenship, and guaranteed equal protection and due process of law. Two years later, the Fifteenth Amendment guaranteed that the "right of citizens of the United States to vote shall not be denied or abridged . . . on account of race, color, or previous condition of servitude."

Well before Reconstruction ended in 1877, the states of the former Confederacy began resisting the extension of civil rights to African Americans. In 1870, Tennessee passed the first "Jim Crow" laws, segregating African Americans from whites on trains, in depots, and on wharves. Congress responded in 1875, guaranteeing African Americans equal rights in transportation, restaurants and inns, theaters, and on juries in what was the nation's first Civil Rights Act. But the legislation could not survive a Supreme Court challenge in 1883, when the justices determined that Congress could not outlaw racial discrimination by private individuals and organizations. This ruling paved the way for southern states to ban African Americans from white hotels, barbershops, restaurants, theaters, and other public accommodations. By 1885, most southern states had also mandated segregated schools.

"Southern Justice," American cartoon by Thomas Nast, 1867.

In 1896, the Supreme Court's ruling in *Plessy v. Ferguson* legitimated segregation, finding that the Fourteenth Amendment did not require "enforced commingling of the races." A lone dissenter took issue, arguing that "separate but equal" would only "stimulate aggression, more or less brutal and irritating" against the rights of blacks.

The assault on African Americans' civil rights was every bit as aggressive in the political arena. Throughout the South, the Democratic Party employed an array of tactics to prevent black voters from voting. In 1890, an amendment to the Mississippi constitution imposed a tax that each black adult had to pay to vote and take a literacy test; South Carolina (1895) and Louisiana (1898) soon followed. By 1910, constitutional provisions in North Carolina, Alabama, Virginia, Georgia, and Oklahoma also effectively barred African Americans from voting. The Republican Party, traditionally supportive of black rights,

W.E.B. Du Bois, after a photograph, ca. 1910.

meekly agreed to the prevention of the black vote. By 1900, the South's African American population was more powerless than at any time since the abolition of slavery.

Nothing better illustrates this than the wave of lynchings that swept the South. Often justified as a response to rarely proven accusations of the rape of white women, the epidemic of lynchings dehumanized blacks and revealed white fears about the consequences of social equality. Between 1880 and 1930, 3,320 blacks were lynched, 95 percent of them in the South. In 1889, Ida B. Wells launched an antilynching campaign, using her skills as a journalist to document these deadly incidents. The campaign against lynching extended well into the 20th century, becoming a national effort that engaged blacks and whites alike.

Wells' response to lynching was an early instance of the activism that would characterize the civil rights movement of the 1960s. Two of her contemporaries—Booker T. Washington and W.E.B. Du Bois—offered opposing responses to the diminishing circumstances of black Americans. Washington, born a slave, embraced a compromising strategy and argued that economic cooperation should replace political conflict. The key to progress was industrial education: "Cast down your bucket where you are,"

A NAACP-sponsored parade in New York City, 1917.

he urged southern blacks. "Cast it down in agriculture, mechanics, in commerce, in domestic service, and in the professions."

Chief among the critics of Washington's appeasing policies was the Massachusetts-born Du Bois, the first African American to earn a Ph.D. from Harvard University. He urged African Americans to utilize "every civilized and peaceful method . . . [to] strive for the rights which the world accords to men" and to cling "unwaveringly to those great words . . . 'We hold these truths to be self evident, that all men are created equal, . . .' " In 1909 he was one of the founders of the National Association for the Advancement of Colored People (NAACP).

The NAACP's initial efforts to fight against segregation, discrimination, and racism were modest. The First World War created jobs for many blacks and generally heightened African Americans' expectations for the postwar period. In 1919, when the white community quickly dashed these hopes, the Red Summer witnessed race riots in over 30 cities, including Charleston,

Memphis, New Orleans, Baltimore, New York, Chicago, and Philadelphia. The resulting repression stalled black progress, largely eliminating the NAACP throughout the South and confining it to a few northern urban centers.

The hostile racial climate of the 1920s and 1930s led many blacks to work for short-term improvements within their segregated sphere without abandoning the ultimate goal of full citizenship. African Americans found that they could endorse the call for equal rights while pursuing white support for improvements to black lives, such as better health care. Efforts to gain traction in the world of labor met only limited success. While some African Americans flirted briefly with communism, others sought positions such as a postal worker, longshoreman, and Pullman porter, all of which provided protection from white retaliation. One such man, A. Philip Randolph, emerged as a powerful spokesman for the Brotherhood of Sleeping Car Porters and, with the 1932 election of Franklin Delano Roosevelt, found a sympathetic ear in the White House.

Eager to derail Randolph's call for a March on Washington in 1941, President Roosevelt issued Executive Order 8802, the nation's first federal effort to prevent employment discrimination and encourage equal opportunity. But the federal government's overall effort to address black civil rights during World War II was weak. Demands for equality within the military were largely unmet, and the Roosevelt administration operated as if it had more to lose by alienating whites than it had to gain by answering blacks' concerns. One new civil rights advocacy group did emerge from the wartime period. In 1942, an interra-

"Together We Win," biracial unity poster, World War II.

cial group dedicated to nonviolent resistance came together in Chicago to form the Congress of Racial Equality (CORE). Initially focused in urban centers in the Northeast, Midwest, Mid-Atlantic, and West Coast regions, in the 1960s CORE would organize campus chapters in the South and would play an important role in the civil rights movement.

While there was no repeat of the Red Summer of 1919, several incidents of postwar violence captured President Harry S Truman's attention. In 1946, he created the President's Committee on Civil Rights, which, after a year's study, issued a series of policy recommendations aimed at the "elimination of segregation, based on color, creed, or national origin." In 1948, Truman continued his assault on discrimination, issuing Executive Order 9981 to desegregate American armed forces. But the president's civil rights initiatives proved too progressive; a coalition of southern Democrats and northern Republicans defeated his legislative effort.

Since the late 1930s, the court system had proven more agreeable than the political arena to the cause of black civil rights. Under the leadership of Charles H. Houston and Thurgood Marshall, the NAACP had adopted a legal strategy that pressed for equality within the Jim Crow system, convinced that the costs of maintaining two truly equal systems of education, for example, would prove too costly to maintain. During the late 1930s and the 1940s, an impressive string of courtroom victories emboldened the NAACP to take direct aim at the doctrine of "separate but equal."

In May 1954, a unanimous Supreme Court determined that segregated schools were in violation of the U.S. Constitution, thereby overturning the 60-year precedent established by *Plessy v. Ferguson*. Unfortunately, the ruling placed responsibility for implementing the decision on the plaintiffs and virtually invited resistance throughout the South. By September, for example, Mississippi had abolished all public schools and established private segregation academies for white students. The following spring, the state legislature passed a law threatening white students who attended school with blacks with jail and fines. And in early 1956, the entire congressional delegations from the states of Alabama, Arkansas, Georgia, Louisiana, Mississippi, South Carolina, and Virginia were among the 100

American civil rights advocate Rosa Parks is fingerprinted by Lt. Drue H. Lackey.

signatories of the Southern Manifesto, which pledged massive resistance to school integration.

On December 1, 1955, the arrest of Rosa Parks, the 42-year-old secretary of the Montgomery chapter of the NAACP, for refusing to give up her seat on a city bus launched a concerted battle against segregation on public transportation. The successful yearlong boycott demonstrated the power of mass action by an independent, self-sufficient black middle class. If *Brown v. Board of Education* had marked the legal turning point in the campaign for African Americans' civil rights, then the Montgomery bus boycott surely marked an even more important psychological turning point.

The boycott also marked the emergence of a charismatic new leader. The Rev. Dr. Martin Luther King, Jr., brought to the civil rights movement

Reverend Martin Luther King, Jr., speaking at Selma, Alabama, 1965.

the prestige traditionally accorded ministers in the southern black church as well as an empowering faith in God's providence. Early in 1957, he assumed leadership of the Southern Christian Leadership Conference (SCLC), a new organization formed to encourage mass action throughout the South. That same year, Arkansas Governor Orval Faubus called out the National Guard to block nine black students from attending Little Rock Central High School. President Eisenhower federalized the National Guard and ordered additional U.S. Army troops to ensure the safe enrollment of the Little Rock Nine, but Faubus' defiance was a reminder of how ingrained resistance to school integration was.

The SCLC embraced a strategy of nonviolent protest that owed much to Indian leader Mahatma Gandhi's fight for Indian independence. Dr. King correctly perceived that continued segregation depended on the everyday compliance of blacks and the widespread belief that racial discrimination was so deeply embedded in southern life that it could not be rooted out. Dr. King believed a movement calculated to provoke violent responses from the white community would break that link and ultimately destroy Jim Crow.

In 1960, few Americans could have predicted that within 10 years the civil rights movement would dismantle a century-old system of social, political, and economic controls that had condemned millions of black Americans to second-class citizenship. The events of the next decade included moments of frightful violence and soaring rhetoric as well as an unprecedented investment in social change by thousands of black and white Americans. By 1968, when Dr. King was assassinated in Memphis, the movement he embodied had broken the back of southern segregation.

Black college students were first to enlist in the fight. In February 1960, four young men denied service at a Woolworth's lunch counter in Greensboro, North Carolina, simply refused to leave. Soon sit-ins were cropping up in Nashville, Richmond, Houston, Atlanta, and other cities throughout the South. By year's end, as many as 70,000 students had participated in a movement that, despite the skepticism of older blacks, had desegregated lunch counters throughout the region.

The success of the sit-in campaigns emboldened a younger generation of African Americans, some of whom chafed under Dr. King's leadership. This emerging generational rift led to the formation of the Student Nonviolent Coordinating Committee (SNCC) in April 1960. Although the SCLC and SNCC would clash over tactics and leadership, both agreed that confrontation and direct action were preferable to the more conservative strategy of litigation long embraced by the NAACP.

During May 1961, a succession of confrontations between the Freedom Riders and southern mobs riveted the nation. On May 4, an interracial group of 13 men and women organized by CORE boarded two buses in

Sit-in at a whites-only Woolworth's lunch counter in Greensboro, North Carolina, 1960.

Mississippi National Guard escorts Freedom Riders traveling on an interstate bus, 1961.

Washington, D.C., determined to test the Court ruling outlawing segregation in interstate transportation terminals. As they neared Anniston, Alabama, a mob attacked and burned one bus and beat some of the riders. When the second bus reached Birmingham, police stood by while the Freedom Riders were beaten once again. A second group of 10 riders that arrived to continue the journey met the same violent reception when they arrived in Montgomery on May 20. The following night, an angry mob surrounded the city's First Baptist Church, where Dr. King and other luminaries were honoring the Freedom Riders. Only the reluctant dispatch of federal marshals to the scene by Attorney General Robert Kennedy defused the potentially explosive situation.

Rejecting Robert Kennedy's call for a cooling-off period, CORE, SNCC, and the SCLC coordinated more than 60 rides during the summer and early fall. Most ended in Jackson, Mississippi, where every rider was arrested. Many were sent to the notorious Parchman Farm, which at one point held 300 Freedom Riders. Late in September, the Interstate Commerce

Commission took steps to enforce desegregation in interstate travel. All interstate buses were to display a certificate that read, "Seating aboard this vehicle is without regard to race, color, creed, or national origin."

September witnessed further violence when U.S. Supreme Court Justice Hugo Black ordered state officials to admit James Meredith as the University of Mississippi's first black student. Three days of rioting caused two deaths and over 300 injuries, many of them to National Guard and regular army troops and the federal marshals charged with protecting Meredith. By the time he graduated the following August, he was still under the 24-hour protection of hundreds of troops.

In December, the movement's attention shifted to the fight against segregation in Albany, Georgia, but an eight-month campaign of massive protest failed to win major concessions from the city government. Albany's wily chief of police fought nonviolence with nonviolence, protecting demonstrators against mob attacks while jailing them again and again. Dr. King, arrested twice, spent 16 days in the local jail.

Police dog attack during Youth Mass Demonstration in Birmingham, Alabama, 1963.

In the name of the greatest people that have ever trod this earth, I draw the line in the dust and toss the gauntlet before the feet of tyranny, and I say, segregation now, segregation tomorrow and segregation forever.

—Alabama Governor George Wallace
Inaugural Address, January 14, 1963

By the beginning of 1963, the civil rights movement had reached a turning point. Dr. King and his lieutenants had come to the conclusion that only tension and crisis seemed likely to produce the gains they sought. Over the next 12 months their actions would produce some of the most iconic moments in 20th-century American history.

Beginning in April, Dr. King and the Rev. Fred Shuttlesworth launched daily mass demonstrations protesting segregation in Birmingham. Arrested on April 12, Dr. King used his time in jail to draft the "Letter from a Birmingham Jail," which combined a powerful reply to his critics with a demand for equal rights. In early May, a series of marches labeled the "Birmingham Children's Crusade" led to the arrest of over a thousand children over a three-day period. "Bull" Conner, the city's commissioner of public safety, loosed fire hoses and police dogs on the marchers. Images of these visually dramatic confrontations quickly spread around the world. On May 10, Dr. King was able to announce an end to the demonstrations in return for the rollback of segregation in many Birmingham businesses and public accommodations. By year's end, similar campaigns in over 300 cities

Martin Luther King, Jr., "I Have a Dream" speech, Washington, D.C., 1963.

across the South had integrated stores, restaurants, and other facilities that had previously denied African Americans service.

On June 11, the same day that Alabama Governor George Wallace dramatically failed to block the enrollment of two black students at the University of Alabama, President John Fitzgerald Kennedy used a televised address to a joint session of Congress to call for civil rights legislation. Long a reluctant participant in the battle for African American rights, the president now declared, "Those who do nothing are inviting shame as well as violence. Those who act boldly are recognizing rights as well as reality." In response to the administration's introduction of legislation a few days later, civil rights organizations joined with labor and religious groups in a call for a March on Washington in support of "jobs and freedom."

I have a dream that one day this nation will rise up and live out the true meaning of its creed: "We hold these truths to be self-evident, that all men are created equal."

—"I Have a Dream" speech
Dr. Martin Luther King, Jr.
Washington, D.C., August 28, 1963

More than 250,000 men, women, and children gathered in front of the Lincoln Memorial on August 28 to hear remarks by prominent civil rights advocates and musical performances by Mahalia Jackson, Marian Anderson, and others. The day's climactic moment came when Dr. Martin Luther King, Jr., rose to deliver one of American history's greatest speeches. "I have a dream today," he proclaimed; a dream that one day "this nation will rise up and live out the true meaning of its creed," a dream that "my four little children will one day live in a nation where they will not be judged by the color of their skin but by the content of their character."

Less than three weeks later, a cruel reminder of how far the country had to travel to realize Dr. King's dream was made painfully apparent. The bombing of Birmingham's 16th Street Baptist Church on September 15

African Americans protest segregation of schools in St. Louis, Missouri, 1963.

killed four young girls and injured 22 others. When combined with the Birmingham campaign, the March on Washington, and the November assassination of President Kennedy, the church bombing added new momentum to the call for passage of the slain president's civil rights initiative.

The following June, President Lyndon Baines Johnson signed the Civil Rights Act, which banned discrimination in employment, federally assisted programs, public facilities, and public accommodations. The law also empowered the federal government to sue southern school districts to force integration, established the Equal Employment Opportunity Commission, and created a Community Relations Service to mediate racial problems. As was the case with the *Brown v. Board of Education* decision, however, there was little provision for enforcement of many of the act's provisions. The act also failed to enable blacks to vote and to protect them from violence. These would become the focus of the 1964 Mississippi Freedom Summer.

Access to public accommodations was meaningless to Mississippi's largely rural black population. Access to the voting booth was far more important. With the support of the Voter Education Project, a SNCC-led pilot project held an alternative election for the Mississippi governorship in which over 80,000 black Mississippians participated. By the following year, a well-entrenched cadre of SNCC volunteers was in place to oversee a major voter education and registration effort.

Violence disrupted the campaign almost immediately. On June 21, 1964, James Chaney, a black CORE activist from Mississippi, and Andrew Goodman and Michael Schwerner, two white volunteers from New York, disappeared after having been briefly arrested. Their disappearance and the discovery of their bodies on August 4 drew massive press coverage to the summer's effort to register black voters. While the voter registration project did not add large numbers of blacks to the Mississippi voting rolls, as many as 40 "Freedom Schools" taught over 3,500 students subjects such as black history and constitutional rights. And the newly created Mississippi Freedom Democratic Party (MFDP) elected a slate of delegates to challenge the seating of the all-white Mississippi representatives at the Democratic National Convention. While the MFDP was not seated, it provided a national television audience with a close-up of the grip white supremacy still had on Mississippi.

The fight to enfranchise black voters continued to be met with violence in 1965. On "Bloody Sunday," March 7, Alabama state troopers viciously beat civil rights workers trying to cross the Edmund Pettus Bridge to march from Selma to Montgomery on behalf of voting rights. Two days later, Dr. King led a second march that crossed the bridge but then turned back to

Voting rights march from Selma to Montgomery, Alabama, 1965.

obey a federal injunction against proceeding. Within a week of this second march, President Johnson stood in the well of the House of Representatives and called for the passage of a voting rights act, closing his speech with the stirring promise that "We shall overcome."

The 1965 Voting Rights Act provided federal oversight and enforcement of voter registration in states and individual voting districts with a history of discriminatory tests and underrepresented populations. It prohibited discriminatory practices that prevented African Americans and other minorities from registering and voting, and forbade electoral systems from diluting their vote. Passage of this law did more to advance the cause of black civil rights than any other single act.

Only five days later, the nation received a stark reminder that black discontent was not exclusively a southern phenomenon. Accusations of police brutality sparked five days of rioting in the Watts neighborhood of South Central Los Angeles, leading to 34 deaths, 1,032 injuries, 3,438 arrests, and over $40 million in property damage. While the inequities endured by African Americans living outside the South were often far more difficult to illuminate than those that had proven so oppressive in the South, they were no less real and ultimately far more resistant to the tactics of nonviolent protest.

No incident better illustrated northern hostility toward the civil rights movement than the failure of the Chicago Freedom Movement. Rallies, marches, and a list of demands for sweeping changes in housing and other governmental practices unfavorable to black interests met fierce resistance. Although the campaign did spur the passage of the Fair Housing Act in 1968, the immediate gains were minimal. But the campaign opened Dr. King's eyes to the reality that racism in the North was far more deeply embedded than he had imagined, and also far less susceptible to moral persuasion. Even in Alabama and Mississippi, he would note, activists had not encountered mobs as hostile to black civil rights as those in Chicago.

By late 1966, the always-uneasy alliances among the SCLC, SNCC, and CORE had begun to fray. Some activists were becoming increasingly disillusioned with the movement's nonviolent mantra, and Dr. King himself was beginning to address issues such as the Vietnam War, which for some seemed unrelated to the core cause of civil rights. In June, Stokely Carmichael, a former Freedom Rider and field operative who was now chairman of SNCC, gave a speech spotlighting "black power" as an alternative approach to civil rights advocacy.

The Black Power movement was, in part, an outgrowth of the civil rights movement's successes. As legal equality was secured, blacks needed to unite and organize effectively to maximize their political and economic power. Black power meant more than just fighting racial segregation, it was a way to attack America's systemic racism. Carmichael called for the SNCC to expel its white members and rejected nonviolence. Others such as Huey P. Newton and Bobby Seale, who founded the Black Panther Party in Oakland, California, in October, lent a far more militant meaning to the slogan.

On April 4, 1968, while in Memphis, Tennessee, to advocate on behalf of striking sanitation workers, Dr. Martin Luther King, Jr., fell victim to an assassin's bullet. Over the next four days riots broke out in Chicago, Washington, D.C., Baltimore, Louisville, Kansas City, and more than 150

Barack Obama, 44th president of the United States.

U.S. cities. The public disorder, which Dr. King would have detested, had scarcely ended when, on April 11, President Johnson signed the Civil Rights Act of 1968, the last great piece of legislation in the fight to extend civil rights to African Americans. It banned discrimination on the basis of race, creed, or national origin in the sale, rental, and financing of housing. It also contained the nation's first "hate crime" statute.

The civil rights movement did not end with King's death, but his absence left a leadership void that would never be satisfactorily filled. Several tried, but none possessed his combination of strategic acumen, messianic vision, and stirring rhetoric. With segregation effectively broken, and federal legislation in place to guarantee the vote and equal access, the challenges for black Americans have become more subtle, less visible, and the solutions remain more elusive. Poverty, the mass incarceration of young black men, renewed challenges to voting rights, and the racism that still sours American society continue to challenge our effort to establish a society that holds "that all men are created equal." The 2008 election of Barack Obama as the nation's first African American president and his reelection four years later were heartening reminders of just how far the United States had come in realizing the Founders' vision. Yet as today's chant of "Black lives matter" reminds us, the fight for African American civil rights is far from finished.

The following National Park Service sites interpret different aspects of the struggle for civil rights. For more information on these sites, please visit www.nps.gov.

African American Civil War Memorial

This memorial honors the service and sacrifices of more than 200,000 African American soldiers and sailors who served to keep our nation whole.

Brown v. Board of Education National Historic Site

The story of *Brown v. Board of Education*, which ended legal segregation in public schools, is one that changed both national and social policy.

Cane River Creole National Historical Park

Secession, Civil War, and Reconstruction brought about many changes in the Cane River area, politically, economically, and socially.

Frederick Douglass National Historic Site

Douglass spent his life fighting for justice and equality for all people, whether black, female, American Indian, or immigrant.

Little Rock Central High School National Historic Site

Nine African American students' persistence in attending the formerly all-white school was an example of the implementation of *Brown v. Board of Education*.

Maggie L. Walker National Historic Site

Maggie Walker devoted her life to civil rights advancement, economic empowerment, and educational opportunities for African Americans and women.

Martin Luther King, Jr. Memorial

Martin Luther King, Jr.'s inspiration broke the boundaries of intolerance as he became a symbol recognized worldwide in the quest for civil rights.

Martin Luther King, Jr. National Historic Site

This site preserves the home of King's birth and the neighborhood where he grew up during an era of racial segregation.

Mary McLeod Bethune Council House National Historic Site

Mary McLeod Bethune demonstrated the value of education and the wise and consistent use of political power in striving for racial and gender equality.

National Underground Railroad Network To Freedom

This site commemorates the stories of the men and women who risked everything for freedom and those who helped them.

Nicodemus National Historic Site

Formerly enslaved African Americans left the South at the end of the post-Civil War Reconstruction period to experience freedom in the "promised land" of Kansas.

Port Chicago Naval Magazine National Memorial

An explosion here killed 202 African Americans working for the racially segregated military. The tragedy became a catalyst for the Navy to desegregate following World War II.

Selma To Montgomery National Historic Trail

Nonviolent supporters led by Dr. Martin Luther King, Jr., fought for the right to vote in Central Alabama. You can trace their march toward freedom on this 54-mile trail.

Tuskegee Airmen National Historic Site

The Tuskegee Airmen overcame segregation and prejudice to become one of the most respected fighter groups of World War II.